101
meditations

101
meditations

selected from

wisdom to
heal the
earth

Meditations on the teachings
of the Lubavitcher Rebbe,
RABBI MENACHEM M. SCHNEERSON
זצוקללה"ה נבג"מ זי"ע

BY TZVI FREEMAN
Author of Bringing Heaven Down To Earth

EZRA
PRESS

Published by Ezra Press
New York
5780 - 2019

101 Meditations

Copyright © 2019 by

718-735-2000
editor@chabad.org

Published by
Ezra Press
770 Eastern parkway, Brooklyn, NY 11213
718-774-4000 / Fax 718-774-2718
editor@kehot.com

Order Department
291 Kingston Avenue, Brooklyn, NY 11213
718-778-0226 / Fax 718-778-4148
www.kehot.com

EZRA PRESS is an imprint of Kehot Publication Society.
The Ezra logo is a trademark of Kehot Publication Society.

ISBN 978-0-8266-9009-8

Printed in the United States of America

foreword

Following the success of *Wisdom to Heal the Earth*, and by popular demand, we are making available a sampling of its succinct meditations in a portable, perhaps more personal format. *Wisdom to Heal the Earth* contains 385 meditations, and this volume, as the title implies, offers *101 Meditations*—in addition to several short essays.

May we very soon merit to greet the Moshiach, who will "heal and perfect the entire world to serve G-d in harmonious union."[1]

Chabad.org

Erev Shabbat Shuva, 6 Tishrei, 5780
Brooklyn, NY

[1] Maimonides' *Mishneh Torah*; Laws of Kings 11:4

how to use this book

Start small. That's how all of life begins. And it's often the best strategy as life continues.

So here's a small book, a sampling of a much larger book titled *Wisdom to Heal the Earth*. Sip this book in little by little. Whet your thirst, get your mind in sync, and maybe one day you'll feel you want to enter the larger book. You'll savor it all the more for the wait.

The snippets and essays herein are meditations on the wisdom of Rabbi Menachem M. Schneerson, affectionately referred to by Jews everywhere as just "the Rebbe." Rebbe means "my teacher." This book was written in the hope that whoever you are that is reading these words might say, "my Rebbe"—because you will find his teachings illuminating your path in life each day.

These are rarely direct quotations. They are teachings that provided me personally with much clarity and direction. This particular collection reflects the Rebbe's very radical yet traditional, mystical yet pragmatic approach to healing the world, condensed into as few words as possible so we can all carry them around with us.

Everything that's in this volume is available at Chabad.org. There, I hope to continue to update this work, as feedback comes in from my readers, and as I continue to meditate upon these teachings in my attempt to apply them in my own life.

—Tzvi Freeman

table of contents

———◆———

———◆———

tikun

Maybe you've heard of *tikun olam*. It's a phrase thrown around a lot in Jewish circles.

Olam means world, and *tikun*—well, it means all sorts of things. But in this sense, it means "to repair and improve."

So *tikun olam* means "repairing and improving the world," which is what we're here to do.

Because, in case you didn't notice, the world is broken. Even the stuff that looks great isn't anywhere near what it's supposed to be.

Some people say, "That's just the way things are. Live with it."

Others say, "Let the One who made it fix it."

And yet others say, "Escape it."

But Jews say, "Fix it. Whatever you can. Leave behind a better world. Because that's what you're here for."

❖

Where did we get such a crazy idea?

Maybe it's from Genesis, where it says we were "placed in the garden to serve it and protect it."

Or from the ancient Midrash that says, "Everything G-d created in His world was designed to be improved."

But, in most part, the way we think of *tikun olam* today is the end-product of a chain with three crucial links—three Jewish revolutionaries of the spirit: Rabbi Yitzchak Luria, Rabbi Yisrael Baal Shem Tov, and Rabbi Schneur Zalman of Liadi.

Each answered a question. Each answer brought us closer to how we think now.

Ari means "lion." That's the title universally granted to Rabbi Yitzchak Luria. He taught for less than three years in Tzfat, in the Galilean hills of Northern Israel, before his early passing in 1572. Few people have had such impact in such a brief time.

The Ari taught in esoteric terms, employing rich metaphor in complex detail. But if we distill it down, through many distillations, we can tell a story something like this:

In the beginning there shone an infinite light. But within an infinite light there can be no finite world.

So the light receded, remaining infinite, but creating a vacuum. Absolute darkness.

And then, from the infinite light beyond and into the darkness within burst a fine, measured beam of light. A ray of conscious thought. An idea. A ray that held everything, all of time and all of space, all wisdom and all understanding of that wisdom, all greatness and might, beauty and glory, wonder and creativity, every voice that would ever be heard, every daydream that would fleet through a distracted mind, every furious wave of a stormy sea, every galaxy that would erupt into being, every charge of every electron, the frantic ant running across the pavement beneath your feet, the basket some kid scored in a park somewhere just now—everything that ever would be and could be, all cocooned within a single, deliberate and conscious thought.

An intense thought. So intense, that each concept it held left no room for anything other than itself.

Which is why that thought is called the *World of Tohu*—meaning: a world of confusion. A world comparable to the emotions of a child—when there is love, there is no room for disdain; when there is anger, there is no room for understanding; when there is self, there is no room for other. A world, as the *Zohar* describes, where each entity is a king, and no other entity is allowed entry until that king dies.

In the language of Kabbalah: Wisdom left no space for Understanding, and Understanding had no room for Wisdom. Kindness left no space for Judgment, and Judgment had no room for Kindness. Each concept was a world of its own, a totality that neither needed nor could bear anything outside of itself. All were ideals. Nowhere was there harmony.

And so that thought exploded.

The explosion gave birth to many worlds. Worlds of *Tikun*. Each world repaired itself, creating its own harmony.

Until it came to our world. In our world, the most vital fragments of Tohu are found, those that the higher worlds were not capable of harmonizing. That was left up to us. Our souls were placed within bodies in this world to perform the ultimate repair.

———◆———

You've heard of a primal explosion before—the Big Bang. But here we are talking about more than matter and energy.

The universe contains conscious beings, such as ourselves. From where does that consciousness emerge, if not from the very fabric of the universe itself?

So think of a primal, singular, deliberate and conscious thought, too intense to contain itself. What happens when such an idea, rather than gradually developing and expanding, chaotically explodes?

Imagine taking a book and casting the words and letters into the air.

Imagine an orchestra where none of the musicians can hear one another, and the conductor is nowhere to be found.

Imagine a movie set without a director, each actor speaking lines without a clue of their meaning.

That is our world. A book in search of its meaning, an orchestra in search of its score, actors in search of their playwright and director.

Awaiting us to rediscover that meaning. To put Humpty Dumpty back together again.

The fragments of that shattered origin are called sparks. They are the divine meaning of each thing—their place and particular voice in the great symphony.

Each spark is trapped within a shell. They are the noise and dissonance that shrouds those sparks when they are thrown violently from their place.

Our job is to see past the shell and discover the spark within. And then to reconnect that spark to its place in that grand original vision.

We call that purification. And the result is called *geulah*—liberation.

The liberation of humankind is intimately tied to the liberation of those sparks of meaning. Your personal liberation is tied to the particular sparks assigned to your soul.

Once a critical mass of sparks has been reconnected, the entire world is liberated. It becomes a different world. An improved world. Because only through that shattering and reconnecting do the parts find their harmony.

This was all very counter-intuitive for a lot of people.

Both religion and philosophy had allotted human beings a passive role in their world's destiny. The Creator had made a beautiful world, we had messed it up. It was up to Him to judge, reward, punish, and take care of our mess.

And now that was reversed. The Creator was the One who had handed us a mess—so that we could complete the job of perfecting it from within. It is a good world, a very good world—essentially because we are empowered to make it good.

Effectively, the Ari gave center-stage to the actions of human beings.

The idea of *tikun* seeped rapidly into every facet of Jewish thought and affected every Jewish movement, directly or indirectly. Jews no longer saw themselves as passive servants of G-d's judgment, but as active players, whose redemption, and the redemption of the entire world—indeed, the entire cosmos—lay in their hands.

Every mitzvah they did gained new meaning. Every prayer, every word of Torah study—each was now not just a good deed to be rewarded, but another step towards the ultimate *geulah* of the entire world.

The Ari was a halachist—an expert and authority in Jewish law—

and he saw all of Jewish practice as a crystallization of Kabbalah. *Tikun* in action.

The idea of *tikun* also spread to the intelligentsia of 17th century Europe, who were fascinated with all things Hebrew, and especially the Kabbalah. It was at that time that people first began to speak in terms of human progress, of building a better world through social action and advances in the natural sciences.

As historians have pointed out, it is difficult to identify any source for these notions—certainly not in Greco-Roman philosophy, nor in the doctrines of the Reformation—nowhere other than the Kabbalah, and specifically the teachings of the Ari.

The idea of *tikun* entered the world through the Ari, but it remained the property of mystics and masters. It was widely misunderstood, distorted, and even abused. It took another 170 years before it gained practical application in the life of the everyman.

Rabbi Israel ben Eliezer is popularly known as the Baal Shem Tov ("Master of a Good Name"). He taught that every person is a master of *tikun* in his or her own world.

Not only the seeker and the scholar, but also the simple farmer and the busy merchant. Even the small child.

By his time, the greatest Talmudic scholars and rabbinic leaders were deeply immersed in the teachings of the Ari. But many of them also believed the only way to fix the human body was by breaking it—by fasting and punishing it. And the way to teach the common people was by breaking their spirit, instilling in them a fear of hell.

The Baal Shem Tov provided a subtle but landmark shift of emphasis. It was less about breaking the shell and more about embracing the fruit—and letting the shell fall away on its own.

To the Baal Shem Tov, *tikun* meant finding the good wherever it could be found and celebrating it. His disciples would wander from town to town, observing the heartfelt prayers, the sincere *mitzvot* and the good deeds of the simple folk, and telling them how much G-d cherished them and their deeds.

Wherever a soul travels in this world, the Baal Shem Tov taught, it is led there to find sparks that have been waiting since the time of Creation for this soul to arrive. Without realizing it, this precious soul is purifying the world, with its deeds and words.

Rabbi Schneur Zalman of Liadi lived—as most Jews of the time—in Eastern Europe. Yet the reverberations of the French Revolution rung throughout his world.

Rabbi Schneur Zalman was also a revolutionary, but a traditional one. More than anyone, he was responsible for conveying the teachings of the Baal Shem Tov into the modern world.

Strange as it may sound, by grounding the teachings of the Ari and the Baal Shem Tov in Midrash and Talmud, and ultimately in the language of Jewish practice, he turned the spiritual quest of humankind on its head.

Our mission in life, he taught, is not to get to heaven. Or to become heavenly beings. It is to bring heaven down to earth.

Earth—not the worlds of angels or the worlds of souls or some reified, divine world of light—but this material world where darkness reigns and truth is hidden. This is the place where the Grand Artist wants to be found.

From the beginning of creation, G-d's presence was
principally in our world, the lowest world.
—*Shir Hashirim Rabbah 5:1.*

Before G-d created this world, He created worlds and
destroyed them, created worlds and destroyed them.
He said, "These I don't like. These I don't like." Then He
created this world. He said, "This one I like."
—*Bereishit Rabbah 3:9.*

Since the time the world was created, G-d desired that
He should have a home among us, the lower beings.
—*Midrash Tanchuma, Nasso 7:1.*

Why would an omnipotent G-d will to dwell in darkness? What desire could He have in a place where He is found only through painful struggle and dogged effort?

The answer is in the process of *tikun* itself:

What happens as we succeed, as we collect those letters and string them back together to form their original words and sentences?

Their collective meaning begins to reappear. A story begins to unfold. An underlying harmony, a symphony—not of our invention, but of our discovery.

What happens when the darkness opposes us? When we persist despite all the lies it spews at us? When we refuse to surrender because we have faith in a deeper truth?

Then a yet deeper light is revealed. One the Author could not say. One that could only be discovered through our stubborn faith and toil.

That is the ultimate light, greater than that which shone at the very beginning. Because we have grabbed the darkness by its neck and forced it to shine more truth than any light could shine.

In effect, the primal thought from which this world was conceived has dissected itself, discovered itself, and put itself back together again.

Tikun, then, does not mean merely repair. In fact, throughout early Jewish literature it rarely does. It means to improve. To fix.

Because in that process, the story discovers not only its own meaning and its own beauty; it discovers its Author. The very essence of its Author that could not be expressed in any spiritual world.

Where? Within itself. Its darkest self.

When you trace *tikun olam* back to its source, you get a whole new picture of what it means. It turns out to be far more revolutionary than you would have imagined.

Tikun olam is about much more than justice and an end to suffering. Those are symptoms. *Tikun* means to fix the cause.

The cause is that we don't know where we are.

We think we are in a world that just is. Or some dark hole to escape.

The first and last step of our *tikun* is to awaken to the realization that we are actors in a great drama, players in a master symphony. That we are here with a mission, accountable to a Higher Consciousness that brought this place into being.

With that awakening alone, the world would be redeemed.

With that awakening alone, we would discover that we never left the Garden. We only lost awareness of where we stand.

We stand within infinite light. For even the darkness is light.

1

the drama

All the cosmos came to be because G-d chose
to invest His very essence into a great drama:
The drama of a lowly world becoming the home
of an infinite G-d. A marriage of opposites, the
fusion of finite and infinite, light and darkness,
heaven and earth.

We are the players in that drama, the cosmic
matchmakers. With our every action, we have
the power to marry our mundane world to the
Infinite and Unknowable.

the game

Like a matching game, each act of beauty uncovers another face of the infinite. Each generation completes its part of the puzzle.

Until the table is set and prepared. Until all that remains is for the curtains to be raised, the clouds to dissipate, the sun to shine down on all our bruised and bloodied hands have planted, and let it blossom and bear fruit.

That is where we are now. We know a world in the process of becoming. Soon will be a world where each thing has arrived.

3

completion

Through many journeys through many lives, each of us will find and redeem all the divine sparks in our share of the world.

Then the darkness that holds such mastery, such cruelty, such irrational evil that it contains no redeeming value—all this will simply vanish like a puff of steam in the midday air.

As for that which we salvaged and used for good, it will shine an awesome light never known before.

The world will have arrived.

write your own script

You came on stage with a script in your hand. The script tells of you, the hero of the story, bringing light into places of darkness, repairing that which is broken, healing that which has fallen ill, creating beauty from scattered fragments of everyday life.

Your soul is tied to that script. Without it, you have no reason to be here. For you were conceived within that context, born to fill that role.

And should you fail to perform according to script, what then?

Then you must write your own script, one that can heal even that which you yourself have broken. A script that can get this story back on track, but this time through a labor of love that belongs to you alone.

And your Creator who conceived you and conceived this entire plan, what will He think of this new script you have composed?

He will laugh in delight, exclaiming, "Look at my child! She has written her own script!"

5

the ultimate delight

What is G-d's ultimate delight?

That a human soul will build portals of light so that the Creator's presence may shine into His creation.

That a breath from His essence will pull herself out of the mud and turn to Him in love.

That a child of His being, exiled to the shadows of a physical world, will discover that the darkness is nothing more than Father hiding, waiting for His child to discover Him there.

But none of these can reach to the essence of all delights, the origin of all things, the hidden pleasure beyond all pleasures:

The delight that this breath, this soul, this child did it all on her own.

if it's broken...

If you see something that is broken, fix it.

If you cannot fix all of it, fix some of it.

But do not say there is nothing you can do. Because, if that were true, why would this broken thing have come into your world?

Did the Creator then create something for no reason?

leave nothing
behind

If it is permissible, we must use it for good.
If it can be raised higher, we cannot leave it below.
If it has become trapped in sinister darkness, the means
will come to liberate it from there.

For everything He made, He made with purpose.

the soul grows up

This soul of yours, ultimately she finds there is something even more momentous than herself. There is her purpose.

To accomplish, to heal, to fix the world—these, she discovers, take precedence over her thirst to return to her womb, to bask in the divine light from which she came.

In that moment of discovery she graduates from being G-d's little child to becoming one with His very being.

9

descending to ascend

The mess of fragments the Creator gave us, those are the pieces He broke apart for us to create our own, better world.

But the mess of fragments we have torn apart ourselves by our own poor choice—who is to say that these too have any redeeming value?

Because this is the way the world was designed: Any descent will eventually result in an ascent. The more broken the world, the better it can be put back together. Yes, a more arduous job on a longer, winding road—but eventually it will be achieved.

Wherever you are, in whatever situation you have gotten yourself, there is purpose, only one purpose: To go higher.

cutting off the supply

To fight evil face-to-face is futile. But we can cut off its supply.

Between good and evil lies a neutral ground, a battlefield—the realm of all things permissible. All supplies to the enemy must pass through this realm. Because evil has no power of its own—it lives entirely off the scraps thrown to it from above.

By taking all that is permissible and using it only for good, honestly and uprightly, with purpose that transcends our own selves, the supply lines are broken.

When every activity of life becomes a way to know G-d, evil simply withers away and dies.

11

fearless

G-d said to Jacob: I am the G-d of your fathers. Do not fear descending to Egypt....

—*Genesis 46:3*

The pain is real. The fear is not.

The pain is real, because we are not in our true place. Nothing is in its true place. It is called exile.

The fear is not real, because no matter where we are, our G-d is still with us.

The only thing we have to fear is that we may no longer feel the pain. For it is that pain of knowing we are in the wrong place that lifts us higher, beyond this place.

12

reporting

He doesn't need you to report on the dirt in His world. He knows quite enough about it, for He put it there—and not because He has an interest in it.

He sent you here to search out the jewels hidden in the mud, clean them and polish them until they shine.

And when you bring them to Him, the angels make a crown of them for Him, and say, "Look what Your children have made for You from the mud!"

13

life's memories

This experience, to give life, to watch it grow, to be torn apart by it, to receive pleasure from it, and to give life again—for this the soul descended from her ethereal heights.

And when it shall return to that origin, enveloped in these memories, it will finally know their depth. And, with them, travel ever higher and yet higher.

14

earned living

All that can be cherished from this world,
All that makes life worth living,
Is that which is mined from its bowels through your own toil,
Fashioned from its clay by your own craft,
Fired in the kiln of your own heart.

The exhilaration that awaited you at the summit of your most
grueling climb.

That for which you bruised your hands and wearied your limbs,
For which you beat back the beast inside you,
For which you defied a mocking world.

Oh, how precious, how resplendent a feast,
a life forged by the hands of its own master!

15

times are changing

The times in which we live are not ordinary times.

Everything is suddenly changing, rearranging itself. Technology leaps ahead daily, affecting the way we do things, how we communicate, our concept of life and the universe.

While an old world struggles to cling to its self-defeating patterns, the stage is set for a world as it is meant to be.

16

inventions

In the beginning, G-d spoke. And whatever He spoke crystallized into material form.

But what about that which He did not speak?

Those waited for the human mind to bring them into being.

When the human being first harnessed fire and bred animals and crops, he simply acted out a divine unspoken thought. The same with those inventors who developed the steam engine, the electric turbine, the radio, and the digital computer. Each creation makes its appearance at the appropriate time, all as choreographed from the beginning of time.

All that G-d made, He made only for His glory, including these. They, too, are vitalized by a spark of the divine. And it is up to us to liberate that spark and reconnect it to its origin, as it is found in the context of the Creator's original plan.

17

technology

Technology is not here simply to provide utility. It is also meant as a springboard to wonder, allowing us to conceive our reality in ways previously unimaginable. It provides an ever-expanding bank of metaphor to crystallize the most abstract ideas into tangible forms.

Don't think that this is a mere side-benefit of technology. On the contrary, for this purpose these ideas were embedded into the universe from the six days of creation, only to be unfolded in our times.

18

freedom out of darkness

Free choice is the quintessential expression of G-d, for He alone is truly free. G-d breathes within the human being, and so we, too, become free to choose our path home.

Darkness, confusion, and the possibility of evil—all this then has a purpose of its own: It provides a stage for us to find G-d within ourselves, seen only when we make the right choice, all on our own.

19

light meets dark

Wherever light radiates, it does not find darkness. For light, darkness does not exist.

Wherever darkness spreads, it does not find light. For darkness, light does not exist.

In a time yet to come, the two shall meet and know one another in perfect union. At that nexus, we will see the One who created all things.

In the meantime, we glimpse a premonition of that wonder. For this is the human being: A breath of the divine within a material body; light and darkness face-to-face within a single being.

mixtures

In this world there is no beauty without ugliness, no joy without sorrow, no pleasure without pain.

You cannot invent a thing that will provide benefit without threat of harm.
Neither is there a human on this earth who does only good without fault.

From the time we ate from the Tree of Knowing Good and Evil, our world became a place of compounds and mixtures.

Wherever you will find another form of good, you will find another sort of evil. Expel that evil, another will take its place. Rare it is, so rare, to find pure and simple goodness in a single being.

Therefore, do not reject any thing for the harm it may render, nor despise any man for the ugliness you find within him.

Rather, use each thing towards the purpose for which G-d conceived it, and learn from each man all the good he has to offer.

21

song and silence

Each thing sings. And each is silent.

Each thing sings, pulsating with the life G-d gives it.

And each is silent. And the silence speaks, saying, "I am. I am just a thing that is."

The silence is also G-d.

For He is the only one who can truly say, "I just am."

22

poor reception

Evil does not descend from above. The transmission from above is pure and coherent. Evil is distortion and noise, an artifact of our reception.

If we would only adjust our reception devices, our attitude and our ability to receive, the signal would become clear.

And that is all of life—adjusting reception.

23

close & dark

When does the moon have no light for us?
When it is closest to the sun.

The closer it comes to alignment between
us and the sun, the more it diminishes in
size. Until, at its closest point, it altogether
disappears. Then, once again, it is renewed and
begins to shine.

At those points in life when we peer into
darkness, groping for some clue why this is
happening to us, where this is taking us, why
we must go through all this—those are the
points of closeness to the light, the points of
renewal.

meaning

What is the meaning?

    The meaning is a story.

A story told before there was any time in which a story could occur:

    Your soul,

a pure child of G-d,

a fractal of the very essence of wisdom,

a breath of life from the innermost source of life,

    will descend from her place,

lower and yet lower,

to clothe herself in a body,

blood and sinews driven by a beast within,

and she will tie her destiny to theirs...

    ...and this body,

along with whatever maddening beast drives that body,

and the entire world in which this soul will dwell,
will do all they can to conceal and negate the light of that divine soul...

...and yet, despite every challenge,
this soul of yours will purify and elevate that body and its beast,
as well as the share of this world to which she has been assigned.

G-d Himself will celebrate in great delight.

Why?
Because the One who transcends all bounds desires to be found in all His essence within our tightly bounded world.

And that will come through us, struggling here with the restrictions and challenges of our world.

And what is the reason He so desires?
There is no reason.
If there were a reason, you would ask, "What is the reason for the reason?"
But this is the desire where all begins.
It is a desire that transcends reason;
it is the place from which all reason is born.
And so it is unbounded and all-consuming.
For it is not a desire of a human being.
It is not a desire of one who has limited will—or of any being or entity at all.

It is a desire that lies at the very core of all being.
That core of being chose to desire,
and now there is nothing else.

———◆———

24

G-d in action

G-d is better grasped in actions than in ideas.

both ways

One who loves must learn fear. One who fears must learn love.

The thinker must do. The doer must think.

The pacifist must fight, the fighter must find peace.

If you flow as a river, burn as a fire. If you burn as a furnace, flow as a river. If you fly as a bird, sit firm as a rock. If you sit firmly, then fly as a bird.

Be a fire that flows; a rock that flies. Love with fear and fear with love.

For we are not fire, nor water, nor air, nor rocks, nor thoughts, nor deeds, nor fear, nor love.

We are divine beings.

26

don't just stand there

As long as you're holding on to where you were yesterday, you're standing still.

27

prison

Torah has no concept of prison as a punishment. Why? Because prison is a futile place. A place where you are told, "You must be in this place, but you must not change what this place is. You will grow older, but you must not take charge of your life. You will live, but you must not give life."

A living human being must effect change in his world, must take charge of his life, must give life to others.

Just as no one can give without receiving, so, too, no one can receive without giving.

28

the parable

The world is a parable, two stories at once;
one story hidden within another.

On the outside, it is the story of a brute
called Reality, a bloodless monster hosting
an army of fiends, beasts, lunacy, and,
worst of all, futility.

On the inside, it is a story of its own
Author with you alone, in eternal love,
and every challenge of this adventure just
another expression of that love, drawing
the two of you yet closer.

The world is a parable, a story on two
channels at once.
On which channel do you choose to spend
your precious time?

29

the river up

When the divine light began its awesome descent—a journey to create one world and then a lower world, and yet a lower world, for endless worlds, condensing and compacting infinite power into finite packages, until focused to the fine, crystallized resolution of the nature of this world—it did so with purpose: to bring forth a world of continuous ascent.

Since that beginning, not a day has passed that does not transcend its yesterday.

Like a mighty river rushing to reach its ocean, no dam can hold it back, no creature can struggle against its current. If we appear to fall backward, to take a wrong turn, to lose a day in failure—it is only an illusion, for we have no map to know its way. We see from within, but the river knows its path from above. And to that place above all is drawn.

We are not masters of that river— not of our ultimate destiny, nor of the stops along the way, not even of the direction of our travel. We did not create the river—its flow creates us. It is the blood and soul of our world, its pulse and its warmth.

Yet of one thing we have been given mastery: Not of the journey, but of our role within it.

How soon will we arrive? How complete? How fulfilled? Will we be the spectators? Or simply the props?

Or will we be the heroes?

a light for 100

A dish of food fills one stomach, but the next in line is still hungry.

Even the warmth of a furnace must be turned higher if more freezing souls appear.

But a light that guides one person will guide a hundred.

Be that light.

come of days

And Abraham was aged, having entered into days.
—Genesis 24:1

Abraham, we are told, did not just age, but "entered into days." Meaning, he had brought all of himself into every one of his days.

Within each moment of life, whatever it was he needed to do, he invested his entire being.

And so he owned every day of his life. His life was his.

32

counting time

We count time as though it were money. But in what way is it so?

We can make more money, but we can't make more time.

Money can vanish in multiple ways, but time can neither be stolen nor lost.

Every penny of our money can be spent or saved, invested or loaned, but time—the hours slip through our fingers, allowing us not the slightest mastery over their incessant stream.

Yet time relies upon us to count its moments.

Because if a moment enters and is wasted, it has come and gone without meaning. And without meaning, in what way did it exist?

A coin uncounted is a wasted coin. A moment uncounted is a moment that never was.

33

life in a day

Before you were formed in the womb, your days were numbered and set in place. They are the chapters of the lessons you came here to learn, the faces of the wisdom this world has to teach you, the gateways to the treasures this lifetime alone can bestow.

A day enters, opens its doors, tells its story, and then returns above, never to visit again. Never. For no two days of your life will share the same wisdom.

34

arrows of life

*The life of Sarah was one hundred years and
twenty years and seven years, the years of the
life of Sarah*

—*Genesis 23:1*

All of them were equally good.

—*Rashi*

In which direction does your life move? To wherever you
have pointed its arrow.

If the arrow points forever backward, to blame the present
on the past and to script the future accordingly, then what
is to make life worth its pain, the story worth its struggle?

But if the arrow points forward to an unfolding destiny,
then every pain becomes the cracking of a shell, every
travail the shedding of a cocoon; as an olive releasing its
oil to the press, a seedling breaking its path through rock
and soil to reach the sun. What is the pain relative to the
promise it holds?

Therefore, Sarah looked back after 127 years, and all her
days, even the darkest, the weariest, were good and filled
with beauty.

35

living time

People talk about "wasting time," or even "killing time."

Neither term is accurate. Time is not yours that you should waste it. Neither does it have a life of its own that you should take that away.

Rather, time awaits you to give it life.

36

balance

In a rush, in confusion, no one can serve his purpose
upon this earth.

A life of purpose is a delicate balancing act of body and
soul, heaven and earth. It requires two feet firmly upon
the ground and a clear head high up in the air.

Only then are you the master.

In a rush, you are not in control of your world—the world
is in control of you. Place your foot gently on the brakes,
slow down, switch gears from madness to mind.

Reclaim mastery.

37

fire burning fire

Life is fire. We are beings of flames. Mostly, we burn with anxiety, with the angst of survival in a hostile world.

But we can harness our own fire: We can stop, contemplate, meditate, and pray. With these, we fan a different fire, a fire of love for the Infinite Light that lies beyond this world and encompasses all things.

One fire swallows another and we are set free. Liberated from fear, we face the world no longer as slaves, but as masters.

four gates

Judges and officers shall you appoint in all your cities....

—*Deuteronomy 16:18*

Think of yourself as a city. You have four magical gates: The Gate of Seeing, the Gate of Listening, the Gate of Imagining, and the Gate of Speaking.

Magical gates, because an Infinite G-d enters your finite city through these gates. An Infinite G-d who cannot be squeezed within any place or boxed within any definition, but chooses to dress neatly in a wisdom called Torah—and these are your gates by which wisdom may enter.

That is why all the world competes to storm those gates. They want you to see the ugliness they see, hear the cacophony they hear, imagine the nonsense they imagine, and speak without end. And then, you will desire all they desire, and no room will be left in your city for that Infinite G-d.

You only need to master those gates and the city is yours.

39

live clothing

We wear a suit that has a life of its own.

It is knitted of the fabric of words, images, and sounds, mischievous characters that no one else can see—or would care to know.

You, however, hear them day and night, chattering, buzzing, playing their games in the courtyard of your mind. They are the threads and the fabric of the garment of thought that envelopes you.

Leave your thoughts to play on their own, and this garment will take you for a walk to places you never wanted to see.

Grab the controls, master this suit. Provide a script, direct your thoughts—those characters will play along.

Do something quick, because you, after all, are dressed up within them.

keep the windows open

Our souls are the windows through which the world
is filled with light, pores through which it breathes,
channels to its supernal source.

There is no function more vital to our universe, nothing
more essential to its fulfillment, since for this it was
formed.

When we do acts of love, speak words of kindness, and
teach wisdom, those windows open wide.
When we fail, those windows cloud over and shut tight.

It is such a shame, this loss of light, this lost breath of
fresh air. A stain can be washed away, but a moment of
life, how can it be returned?

panic

Panic, confusion, and pessimism, these are the nightmares of a heart freely handed the reins to your mind.

Reverse the process. Hand your mind the reins to your heart.

Feed yourself with wholesome thoughts. With all your willpower, stay focused on those thoughts. Ignore the burning panic in your heart; refuse to allow it to distract you.

Soon enough, the black horse of pessimism gallops off into the night.

G-d's image

We were created in G-d's image. What is G-d's image? It is a vision. A vision that triggered the beginning of time.

From a point before and beyond all things, G-d looked upon a moment in time to be. He saw there a soul, distant from Him in a turbulent world, yet yearning to return to Him and His Oneness. And He saw the pleasure He would have from this reunion.

So He invested His infinite light into that finite image and became one with that image, and in that image He created each one of us.

That vision that He saw, that was the moment now.

43

when is G-d?

G-d is found at two poles of time:

He is found outside of time.
And He is found here within the moment now.

From that point beyond time, G-d looks within the
moment now, and says, "From this, I will have delight."

With that choice, all of past and future is created anew.

44

original success

Before your soul descended to this world, she was destined to succeed. If not in this lifetime, then in another, or yet another—eventually she will fulfill her entire mission. And in each lifetime, she will move further ahead.

It was this knowledge that conceived her.
It was this inspiration that brought the world to be.
It is this vision of her success that lies at the essence of all things.

45

crossroads

There are crossroads where you choose not only your future, but your past as well.

Take one road, and your past becomes but an irrelevant and forgotten dream.

Take another road, and even the darkest past can become a magnificent frame for a moment of glory. The moment for which your soul was formed and all the past was made.

46

first day

All is defined by destiny. Even the past
is redefined by the arrow of its future.
The very existence of that time that held
that past is recreated once it achieves its
hidden destiny. A destiny that only you
can reveal.

That is all that matters: Now, the first day
of all of time—future and past.

happy birthday, universe

Every year, our Sages taught, with the cry of the shofar, the entire universe is reborn.

At that time, with our resolutions and our prayers, we hold an awesome power: To determine what sort of child this newborn year shall be—how it will take its first breaths, how it will struggle to its feet, and how it will carry us through life for the twelve months to come.

In truth, it is not only once a year: At every new moon, in a smaller way, all life is renewed again.

So, too, every morning, we are all reborn from a nighttime taste of death.

And at every moment—in the smallest increment of time—every particle of the universe is projected into being out of absolute nothingness, as it was at the very beginning.

Which is why there is always hope. Because at every moment, life is born anew. And we are the masters of how this moment will be born.

48

time travel

To change the past, there is no need to travel in a time machine. Everything can be done by remote control.

Here's how it works: From beyond the continuum of time, its Creator looks at where your spaceship is heading right now. From that point, He creates all its trajectory—through the future and through the past.

Switch the direction your past is sending you. Soon enough, it becomes a different past.

49

two channels

There are two channels on life's tv. On one plays a fantasy; the other is real life.

The fantasy is a world that imagines itself to be its own truth; where nothing is of intrinsic value, and everything functions by the rules of chance and necessity.

In this world, you are nothing more than another background or shadow, an extra in a plotless movie, a disposable prop for a five-second set.

In this world, life may be prosperous. Or disastrous. Whatever the scene demands, so you shall be given. Until it is time for the next scene to begin.

The real life is a world in which you stand face to face before the Director of this grand drama. But your story is not this drama. It is this intimate relationship of yours with the Director.

All things may change—the props, the backgrounds, the actors, even the play itself—but this is forever. It is truth.

50

heaven desires
earth

There are those who chase all things of heaven—and find they cannot live.

There are those who chase all things of earth. Their life is not worth living.

Heaven desires the earth, and the earth is lost without heaven. Make your life a marriage of the two, as lovers that never part, and you will find peace.

51

beyond wisdom

Do not be misled by those who claim there is no purpose.

They may know life, but not its womb.

They may know darkness, but not its meaning.

They may have wisdom, but they cannot reach higher, to a place
beyond wisdom,
a place from which all wisdom began.

They may reach so high until the very source from which all rivers flow.
To the place where all known things converge, where all knowledge is
one.

But they have not touched the very core of being, the place before
being begins, where it is chosen that being will begin, where there
is nothing—no light, no darkness, no knowledge, no convergence, no
wisdom—

Nothing but the burning purpose of this moment now.

Because it is for that purpose that being began.

52

free choice

Choose life!

—*Deuteronomy 30:19*

We created beings can only know that which is. That which is not, we can only imagine—or exert effort to make it happen.

But imagine a great mind from which thoughts emerge and then crystallize as the events of the physical world—spontaneously, without effort.

All events and all things—all except those matters for which this world was originally brought into being. Those are hidden thoughts—they neither emerge nor crystallize; they only unfold through our choice to do good.

When we choose life, we redeem G-d's subconscious—His most hidden desire.

53

essential good

At the core of all our beliefs lies the
conviction that the underlying reality
is wholly good; that evil lies only at the
surface, a thin film of distortion soon to be
washed away by the waves.

54

the airplane does not yet exist

A large group of visitors were preparing for their flight back to Israel when news came that the Rebbe wished to address them before they would leave. With bags half-packed, they came running to listen, wondering how they would make the flight. The Rebbe spoke at length, seemingly oblivious to the time. And then:

I know it's hard not to glance at the clock. In an hour and a quarter, your plane is leaving. Bags need to be packed, you need to bid farewell to friends and family, you need to be there on time.

But in your reality, the airplane does not yet exist. The tickets do not yet exist. Kennedy Airport does not yet exist. When it comes time for all these things to be dealt with, the Creator will cause them to materialize. All that exists for you right now is this room where we are talking.

Yes, it's hard to live this way, even though we all know it is true. But it is the only way to make the most of your time. There is only so much time in life. Whatever moment you are in, you need to be there and only there.

Because in your world, at that time, nothing else exists.

out in the world

Who is going to fix up this mess of a world? The politicians? The social workers? The philosophers? The think tanks and analysts?

Perhaps some great minds can shed some light so we can find the door. Perhaps some sensible bureaucrat may even leave the door unlocked.

But don't wait for real change to enter through that door. Don't wait for the academics and authorities in their ivory and steel towers to plan or enforce it. Don't wait for those taking notes on the other side of a one-way glass to fix the world.

Real change is an inside job. It is made by those who have an investment in the real world. By people who are charging for their services, buying and selling, inventing and manufacturing, trading and transporting. Those building the world have the power to fix it.

—◆—

Money and *tikun* have much to do with one another. Both are about putting things together. Or people together. Or people and things together.

Somehow, just with those connections, you've created more value in the world. Since you created it, you get a major chunk of that value, often in the form of money.

It turns out that making money is magical—something out of nothing.

How does the magic work? Where does that value come from?

Go back to the idea of *tikun*. Everything began as a single thought. When we make connections, we are reassembling that thought. As the connections assemble, more and more meaning appears.

We see that meaning as value. Sometimes we can even represent that value as money. And with that money, we can make yet more connections.

It turns out that commerce, as well as art, music, literature, the sciences—basically all activities that are particular to the human race—can be a form of *tikun*. They all provide opportunities to connect the shattered fragments of our world to create value.

Now look at our world today. A global communications network in the hands of almost everyone has increased abundance many times over, spreading it to the extreme frontiers of human settlement.

For thousands of years, only a select few—around 5%—were literate. Today 80% of adults around the globe can read and write. Poverty and hunger have diminished worldwide more rapidly than anyone predicted—by more than 50% in twenty years. Despite the common perception, we enjoy the most peaceful era of history—because we've discovered it's better to make commerce than war.

A villager in Botswana may not have electricity, running water, or even a bicycle to ride, but he has a mobile phone, and with that, access to all human knowledge and a means to contribute yet more information and experience. Nothing could more powerfully transform a person's understanding of himself and his relationship to the world.

Connections are being made. Connections that create value.

The problem is that there are other kinds of connections. Connections, paradoxically, that tear us apart.

Tikun is what occurs when people do the things that people do—and do them right. It happens when we connect from the inside-out. When we deal with other people as fellow human beings. When we appreciate the value of the resources we work with. When we take pride in our services. Even more so when we see our work as a divine mission—which it truly is.

When business is not about value, but about money; not about the fruit, but about the shell; not about the people, but about what you can get out of them—then it's a dark and nasty force of chaos, dehumanization, and destruction.

Instead of harmonizing society, so that each makes his or her unique contribution, it renders a granulated, homogenized pseudo-culture—a world where all the traditional bonds of family, community, tribe, and culture are ripped away, to be replaced with isolation, abuse, and emptiness. We are left as chaff in the wind, to be swept in aimless, lonely circles. Nothing sticks, there is no center, there is no value.

So it is that history travels in two opposing trajectories at once, both driven by the same human drive to dominate our world—for better, but too often, for worse.

Who chooses which trajectory will dominate? Not the legislators. Not the academics. Not the preachers. Not the enlightened souls who sit and ponder.

It is the salesperson who sells his customers what he knows to be best for them. The school teacher who treats each child as a person, an entire world. The business executive who is concerned for the welfare of the company's employees both at the office back home and in the factory across the sea—and in the villages in which those workers live. The manufacturer whose every worker feels a sense of mission and meaning in their work.

Where the real world happens, from there is its *tikun*.

There will come a time, writes Maimonides, when "the occupation of the entire world will be only to know G-d." Meaning, we will have occupations. We will be builders. Importers. Exporters. Manufacturers. Professionals. And why will we occupy ourselves with these things? Because these are the ways to know the One who spoke and brought all things into being.

And so they are, as well, today.

———◆———

joseph

And there came a day, and Joseph went to do his
work...   *—Genesis 39:11*

Joseph went to review his accounting books.
                    —Targum Onkelos

Joseph , the tzaddik, went to review his accounting
books?!   *—Torat Chaim, Vayeishev*

Joseph was a soul from the World of Atzilut—a divine world
of pure light entirely beyond any physical or spiritual reality.
A world one with its Emanator.

For Joseph, even as he lived within a body within this world,
there was no world, because the light of his soul shone so
brightly, nothing of this world could exist.

And yet, here Joseph is going to do his work, to review his
accounting books!

It is one thing to be beyond the world, but to be so far beyond
and yet occupied with it, both at once—that is something
absolutely wondrous.

56

working lessons

If all the world is a classroom and all of life is
a lesson, then certainly your profession and
workplace are included.

After all, He has unlimited ways to provide your
livelihood—why did He direct you to this way of life?

What sparks of the divine await you here?

financial planning

Here is how to make an honest living, with confidence and minimal worry:

Determine how much you need to provide for your family needs.

Next, get into a business that can make that sum of money.

Now, put your best foot forward to do whatever needs to be done.

But no more than that. More will get you less.

Then pray for compassion, and trust in the One who provides all life to provide your livelihood as well.

You've put out just the right size bucket in the rain. Now trust that heaven will fill it to the brim.

58

business transformation

There is a beast inside. It awaits you for its *tikun*.

How do you fix up the human beast? First with prayer, then with food, but ultimately by doing business.

You need to start with meditation and prayer, because that beast inside needs to experience not only wonder, but even love for G-d. The problem is, in prayer and meditation, you have not yet met that beast on its own ground.

Next, eat your breakfast like a human being is meant to eat—a step higher than the food you consume, raising it up rather than letting it pull you down. Then, yes, you have met your human beast on its own ground. But not on its own terms. You are still fighting with it—against its desire to be pulled down into the food.

So then go out into the world and provide goods and services of value, and do that with integrity.

No longer are you fighting against the human beast. You are working with it and from within it, with all the talents and skills you have. Because otherwise, you are not providing the value for which others are paying, and that is not integrity.

Now you can understand why the very first question asked of the soul when she returns from her mission in this world is not "How did you pray?" or "How did you eat" but "Did you do business with integrity?" For that is when you truly fixed up this world.

59

worldly occupation

Why must we have jobs? Why can't our bread fall from heaven?

It does. Our bread is manna from heaven. But it bursts forth from Above like a solar flare—a light far too intense for any world to contain.

So, in each world in the chain of spiritual worlds that extend from above to below until our earthly realm, the beings of that world must labor to absorb that light. Only then can the light descend to the world that follows theirs in the chain—and there yet another form of labor is required, according to the limitations of that world.

Until the light arrives at our world. And here we must do the work that our world requires so that it, too, may absorb the light.

And that is why we each have our worldly occupations.

60

simple advice

Ask advice from those with experience.

They will provide you freely that which they acquired at great expense.

61

wall street idol

The ancients looked up at the heavens and gazed at the stars
in their constellations. They honored them as stewards of
divine energy and life, as the embodiment of all forces of
nature and the origin of human passions.

They were wise, but they were fools—they abandoned the
Master for the servant. For in truth there is only One and all
else is but a tool in His hand.

Modern man looks up to the headlines of the finance page and
sees there all the forces that will make or break his career, his
retirement plans, his success as a human being.

He, too, is a fool, for in truth there is only One and all else is
but a tool in His hand.

62

exchange of matter

Separating between your physical needs and your spiritual needs is both counter-productive and futile. The spiritual breathes life into the physical, and the physical rises to become spiritual in a perpetual chemistry of exchange.

Heal the soul and the body is renewed. Heal the body and the soul is empowered.

63

community and the individual

A community that builds itself by quashing the individual is not a community.

True unity and harmony is only achieved when each individual plays his or her unique part, meshing and interlocking together as a single, organic whole.

64

getting real

To know that this world is not some wild jungle where whoever is stronger or richer or smarter can abuse and destroy without regard for those beneath them—this is not a matter of religion or faith, particular to one people or group of believers. This is the underlying reality—that this world has a Master, and that Master is not any of us.

A peaceful society can only endure when it is built upon that which is real and true.

this is good

Who is rich? He who is satisfied with his lot.
—Pirkei Avot 4:1

With each event of life, you have a choice:

You can complain that you didn't get what you deserve; that you have a right to complain, because you are suffering...

...or you can have faith that the One above, who is good and provides only good, is taking care of your life in its every detail...

...because the good that you can perceive is only a limited good, while that which you cannot perceive as good is good beyond your understanding;

...because nothing that G-d provides you with can be bad; all that He does for you He does to lift you closer to Him, with love...

...because your faith that all is truly good heals the world, allowing the hidden good to become obvious good to celebrate in the here and now...

...and then you are rich.

Wealth, it turns out, is all a matter of interpretation.

66

not an angel,
not a beast

If you believe you are an angel, prepare for disappointment.

If you believe you are a beast, you may well become depressed.

Best to know you are human. Stay away from situations you can't handle, and when you fail, pick yourself up, say you're sorry, and continue onward.

That's even higher than the angels.

67

a soft stick

It used to be that the soul fought with the body, until one conquered the other by force.

Then the Baal Shem Tov came and taught a new path: The body, too, could come to appreciate those things the soul desires.

In the place of self-affliction and fasting, the Baal Shem Tov showed his students the way of meditation and joy. Every need of the body, he taught, could provide a channel to carry the soul high.

realistic optimism

*I lift my eyes to the mountains, from whence
will come my help?*

—*Psalms 121:1*

People believe that only fools are optimists. But the
opposite is true.

Precisely because we understand how desperate
the situation really is, how helpless we are, and how
impossible the challenge, that itself tells us how great
a G-d we have—a G-d who can lift us high beyond the
natural order and transform the most ominous darkness
into brilliant good.

The greater a realist you are, the greater your joy.

69

soul-body bonding

The human mind despises the body that houses it,
but the soul has only love.

The mind would soar to the heavens,
but for a body that chains it to the earth.
The mind would be consumed in divine oneness,
but for the body's delusion of otherness,
as though it had made itself.

But the soul sees only G-d.

In that very delusion of otherness,
in that madness of the human ego,
even there, the soul sees only G-d.

For she says, "This, too, is truth.
This is a reflection of the essence of all things,
of that which truly has neither beginning nor cause."

Therefore, she embraces the bonds of the body,
works with the body and transforms the body.
Until the body, too, sees only G-d.

the autograph

When He had finished His world, complete and whole, each thing in its place, the earth below and the heavens beyond,

...it was then that the Artist signed His holy name, a stillness within the busy painting, a vacuum in time, a pocket of silence within the polyphony, so that the Infinite Light could kiss the finite world, enter within and grant it life.

He called that Shabbat.

In each thing there is a Shabbat, a sense of wonder, of knowing that there is something greater, something it will never truly know, and a yearning to receive from there.

With that yearning, it receives life. Without it, nothing can survive. For that emptiness provides entry to the Infinite.

71

natural response

There is an easy path to fulfill the Torah. Not by forcing yourself, not by convincing yourself, but by achieving awareness:

A constant awareness that all you see and hear—the wind that strokes your face, the pulse of the heart beating in your chest and pumping through your veins, the stars shining in the heavens and the hard earth beneath your feet—all things of this cosmos and beyond, all are but the outer garments of a great Inner Consciousness, a projection of His will and thoughts. Nothing more than His words to us, words within which He Himself is found, but concealed.

The Master of that consciousness speaks to you and asks you to join Him in mystic union in your actions, your words, and your thoughts.

In such a state of mind, could you possibly choose otherwise?

72

practice makes perfect

Anyone can come to see a higher world. But it's not a flash of revelation from above that will take you there.

Train yourself, consistently, every day, until you become used to seeing each thing the way it is seen from above.

Real change only comes from consistent, daily practice.

73

G-d within

Before the Baal Shem Tov, people thought of G-d as the One who directs all things from above and beyond. The Baal Shem Tov taught that the vital force of each thing, the place from which comes its personality, its sense of pain and pleasure, its growth and life—that itself is G-d.

Not that this is all of G-d. It is less than a glimmer of G-d. Because G-d is entirely beyond all such descriptions.

Rather, that life force is G-d as He is found within each creature He has made.

does he need our praises?

One time my kids outsmarted me. I had them in the van, and we pulled into a parking lot where a ferris wheel and other rides had been set up. But I had no time to take kids on merry-go-rounds on a hot summer day. I had work to do.

And then I heard from the back seat:

"Oh, thank you, Daddy! You're the best daddy in the whole world! You brought us for a surprise! Yay, Daddy!"

Five minutes later, I was frying on the hot pavement, at the foot of a ferris wheel, waving to my kids.

It was then that I understood a teaching of the Rebbe:

Before we make any request, we praise the Master of the Universe. We praise Him for the beauty of the world He has made. We praise Him for rescuing the widow, the orphan and the oppressed. We praise Him for the simple things, the lowly things, the everyday things that go unnoticed.

In that way, we are bringing Him into our world, and our prayers have an effect in this world.

75

de-kvetching

The more good news you bring your Creator, the less need you will have to complain about the opposite.

Meditate on those things you have to be thankful for. Express your thanks out loud.

The number of things to kvetch about will rapidly diminish.

learn as a child

Intuitively, we imagine the child as a dependent, a pupil, an adult in the making. As though the child is only becoming, not yet being. We invest in the child, not for what the child is now, but for what the child will become.

But the child is now.

If we do not learn from the child, we are not living in the now. We have cut our roots that nurture us from our past. How will we grow into our future?

If we cannot learn from the child, we are not adults. We are old people. We do not grow; we only age.

To grow is to build upon that with which you began. Leave the child within you behind and you are a nomad without a destiny, wandering in circles through shifting sands that leave no trace of your footsteps and only portend your eventual demise.

Listen to the child, learn from the child, and you are a towering tree anchored and nourished by deep roots, forever supple in the wind, sprouting new leaves, twigs, and branches whenever the sun glows.

Because as much as the child needs the adult as a nurturer and a guide, so, too, we adults need the child to return us to our innocence, to the point inside from which we first sprouted, and from where we still receive life. Which perhaps explains why the Rebbe again and again taught us to think as a five-year-old child.

The Mishnah defines wisdom as the capacity to learn from anybody and everybody. For "there is no person who does not have his time, nor any thing that does not have its place."

For the world is a constantly revolving sphere, each point the very pinnacle of that sphere in its unique way. So that there is no being that receives and does not give, just as there is no being that gives without receiving. There is no time in life that is only a preparation for a later time. And there is no person who is only here to become someone else.

A woman is a woman and a man is a man. A teacher is a teacher and a student is a student. An adult is an adult and a child is a child. And yet all of us provide, all of us teach, all of us nurture—each in a way no other can.

This is *tikun*, this is a revolution that is forever: When there are no one-way streets in our world. When each thing finds its purpose in this moment now.

When we can hear the deepest wisdom in the simplicity of the child.

76

ungraspable

All our philosophy is meant only to achieve some sort of grasp of what a small child means when he prays to G-d.

But we can't.

As soon as we grasp, it is gone.

77

learning the child

There are no one-way streets in our world. There is
no one who gives without receiving, and there is no
one who receives without providing something back
in return.

So it is with the child. Just as the adult gives the
child the knowledge and wisdom of life, so the child
shows the adult how to live it to its fullest.

78

childish
teaching

A child cannot learn something without running outside and screaming it to others.

And so it should be with all those who have knowledge.

79

the engaged
child

Watch a child involved in any activity.

Whatever a child is doing, there is the child, the
whole child.

childish demands

When a child feels something is missing, the child wants it, demands it with all his heart and soul—and demands it now.

We are G-d's children.

The world is not the way it should be.
None of us are in our proper place.

We need to demand that He fix all this.

We need to scream out from our hearts, as a small child would scream.

We need to plead that He fix it now.

81

childish enthusiasm

A child's enthusiasm comes in a storm, taking over the child's entire world. That is why, when a child embraces a new, good way of being, it enters forever, and nothing can ever take it away.

82

childish love

A child gives love for the sake of love.

But even an adult can learn to do the same.

83

there with the student

The Talmud states that when a student is exiled, his teacher must be exiled with him. Not simply that he must go with him. He must be exiled with him.

Which tells us: If you truly want to teach, you must put yourself in your student's space.

If your student has wandered far astray, tear yourself away from your own space; feel what it is like to be distant. If your student is in pain, let that pain become your pain. There must be nothing that lies between your student's world and your own.

Teach in this way and you can bring even the most distant student to your own level of understanding. And yet higher: You will learn from this student that which you could never have learned from your own teachers and colleagues.

84

your own tradition

Nobody believed Noah. But Abraham, some say, convinced most of his generation.

Noah spoke as someone who followed a tradition of the past. Abraham described how he had discovered G-d on his own.

You can only give it to others once you have made it your own.

healing begins at home

There's a story about a man who was lowered down a deep shaft, lower and lower, until the darkness was so dark he could touch it with his fingers, the damp so damp it seeped through his bones, and the cold so cold it made those bones shiver. And all around was nothing but mud.

Finally, without warning, he hit the hard rock bottom.

When they pulled him back up, they asked, "What did you find down there?"

"It was cold," he answered.

"What else?"

"It was dark," he answered.

"What else?"

"What else do you want?" he answered. "I hit rock bottom and it was cold, dark, and full of mud!"

"We know it's full of mud!" they retorted. "It's a mine! Now where are the diamonds?"

If you read the introduction to the chapter on *Tikun*, you may have already figured out the story. It's about us, about how our souls come down to a fractured, light-deprived world.

If you don't know why you're here, sometimes all you can see is mud. And there's no shortage of mud in this world.

But if you know you're here on a mission, the supreme mission to rescue the lost divine sparks and repair the universe, and if you know that the most brilliant, precious stones are to be found in the darkest, deepest places—then the mud becomes almost irrelevant. All you see are diamonds.

The first place to look for those diamonds is in your own home. Then in your community.

Once you can find them there, you'll see diamonds everywhere.

———◆———

85

harmonization

Harmony at home is a matter of emphasis:

Let dissonance slip by.

Celebrate beauty.

86

home improvement

Harsh words, demands, and ultimatums—these
shake the very foundations of a marriage and a
home, tearing its walls apart until each person and
each thing stands alone.

Gentle words, understanding words and listening
words are the trunk from which a marriage grows;
the foundation upon which a home stands. This is
the sweet and pleasant path of Torah.

A home cannot be repaired unless its foundation is
firm. Once a couple learns to speak as friends, their
marriage can endure everything, forever.

87

give & take

Marriage is not a power struggle, and the home is not a battlefield. To give in does not mean to relinquish power, and talking things over does not mean you are entering negotiations.

The two of you comprise a single entity—a couple. What is good for one is good for the other. When you make a decision, it is the decision of both of you as one being. Do it not as a sacrifice but as a gift, not as a defeat but as a triumph of love.

home

A home is more than a house; it is a state of being. A home provides space and shelter, not just for bodies, but for the human spirit.

Who creates this space? Mainly, the woman. As it says, "A feminine wisdom builds her home" (Proverbs 14:1).

89

wisdom, not hammers

"A home," wrote Solomon the Wise, "is built with wisdom."

And not with a hammer.

Because wisdom is the glue of beauty. Wisdom, meaning the ability to step back and see all of the picture, the past and—most important—the future to which all this leads. To see the truth inside each thing.

Without wisdom, there are only fragments. With wisdom, there is a whole. And there is peace between all the parts of that whole.

meditation
on a scolding

Before you scold a child, stop and think of who this is and where you stand.

This is a child of the Creator of the Universe.

And you stand before Him, scolding His child.

91

who this
really is

What you see of a person, you may not like.

Yet who this person really is, you can never know.

Speak to that: Look past the outer shell and talk to the unknowable inside.

Talk to the soul, and she will hear.

92

unreacting

The nature of a human being is to simply react, to throw back at others the medicine they mete out to you.

Rava, the Talmudic sage, would say, "Resist the urge to return bad with bad, hurt with hurt, scorn with scorn—and the heavens will overlook your own scorning, your hurting, your acts that were not good."

G-d shadows man. Go beyond your nature with others, and so will He do with you.

93

blind love

The greatest gift of love is to turn a blind eye. The most essential glue of any relationship is the ability of at least one of you to say, "I understand. It's okay. Let's just get on with things."

After all, that is what we continuously say to our own selves out of our self-love. And it is what we would like the One Above to say to us.

94

re-uniting

When man and woman were first formed, they were a single being.

Then G-d divided them apart, so that they could achieve a higher union.

Why is it higher?

Because now it is through their own effort.

That is true oneness: When two choose to be one.

95

getting personal

When does the depth of a relationship become realized? Once it has broken down.

As long as each fulfills the other's expectations, we see only a contract and its transactions. Once trust is breached, a new depth must appear: The depth of the human being.

If there is truly a relationship—if it is the person inside that matters— then there is a search for forgiveness, for return, and for healing.

So it was that within forty days of entering into a contract with the One Above, the Children of Israel broke the deal. And the soul below and the One Above discovered they could not part from one another.

96

forgiveness by the book

When his people broke the deal and incurred divine wrath, Moses told G-d, "Forgive them. And if you do not, erase me from Your book that You have written."

Meaning: "I know You want to forgive them. You love them no matter what. You loved them before, when they had all but abandoned You in Egypt, and You love them now as well. It's only this book that stands in the way. And if so, I want no part of such a book."

It was then that G-d wrote forgiveness into His book.

And so must we.

97

a different peace

True peace is not a forced truce, not a homogenization of differences, not a common ground that abandons our home territories.

True peace is the oneness that sprouts from diversity, the beauty that emerges from a panorama of colors, strokes, and textures, from the harmony of many instruments each playing a unique part, not one overlapping the other's domain by even the breadth of a hair.

Those who attempt to blur those borders, whatever be their motives, are unwittingly destroying the world.

Beginning with the crucial border between man and woman. For this is the beginning of all diversity, the place where G-d's oneness shines most intensely from within His precious world.

constant bonding

Matter and energy are two opposites. Energizing a piece of matter requires a constant flow.

Existence and nothingness are two opposites. Keeping the world in existence demands a constant renewal.

Heaven and earth are two opposites. Infusing the earthly with spirituality requires a constant effort.

Woman and man are two opposites. Therefore, courtship never ends.

reality in untidy boxes

Tell me you found G-d in a tidy package—I will tell you that it is not G-d, it is a product of a clever mind.

Tell me you found G-d in the limitless beyond—beyond space, beyond time. That too is not G-d. That is just a greater mind.

Where the boundless dwells within a bounded space, where darkness shines, silence sings, bitterness is sweet, and a moment lives forever, where a man and a woman live in harmony, an adult learns from a child, a warrior spreads kindness, and enmity subsides to make room for friendship and love,
where the body embraces the soul
and the soul the body,
in the union of all opposites—

there is G-d; there is the essence of all that is real.

100

the path of the humble

If we were truly humble, we would not be forever searching in higher paths on the mountaintops. We would look in the simple places, for the practical things that need to be done.

True, where do these simple, practical things reside? In a transient world, a world of falsehood, a world where people believe they have needs that are not real needs, where they suffer more pain than life truly creates.

In a world where your motives are always in question, where the difference you make is always in doubt. Because it is a world where you cannot give without gaining more than you have given, you cannot love without being loved, you cannot honor without being honored.

Nevertheless, the soul who knows her place knows that this is where the great and lofty G-d can most be found—in a simple act of lending a hand or a whispering a comforting word in a world of falsehood and delusions.

101

imaginary kindness

Most of the favors we do for others are things they do not need, things they only imagine they need, because they live in a world propelled by fantasies.

And most of the kindness we do is saturated with ulterior motives. We do kindness for those we love, those close to us, or those who make us feel good when they receive.

But this does not matter. They are acts of kindness, nonetheless, and G-d desires to be found in acts of kindness. And where can kindness be performed? In a world of delusions, where people imagine all sorts of needs, and each of us is dependent on the other.

The highest, indeed, is found in the lowest, the deepest truths are submerged in the muddiest pits of confusion.

epilogue

By the seventh generation of Chabad, the walls separating the Jew from the rest of the world had all come tumbling down. It was 1951, and the Rebbe, Rabbi Menachem M. Schneerson, accepted the leadership with these words: "We are the generation to complete the work of all the generations before us, to finally bring heaven down to earth."

Until this point, Chabad had been about the soul, the mind and the heart. That was the material world that needed to be fixed.

For the Rebbe, fixing up the material world meant the entire big world out there, every last country, every last culture, every last individual. You could almost say that everything up to this point had been only a rehearsal—battle practice for the final victory. And now, the paratroopers were landing on foreign soil. Everywhere.

It meant sending young couples and their children out to every place a Jew may roam—whether that be Tunisia or Thailand,

Kathmandu or Kentucky. What Rabbi Schneur Zalman of Liadi, the Baal Shem Tov, and the Ari had spoken in the esoteric language of the soul and the heavens suddenly meant here, now, down on this earth. *Tikun* had hit the hard, concrete pavement.

It wasn't just those Chasidic families. The Rebbe asked this of every Jew and every human being with whom he came in contact. The message, always: You have a job to do. The circumstances in which you find yourself, the community in which you live, your place of work and the skills and talents G-d has given you—they are all screaming out to you to do your job. And what is that job? To turn this world on its head.

Neither was the Rebbe satisfied with his impact on the Jewish world alone. He urged Jews to speak with their non-Jewish neighbors and acquaintances, to tell them, "You are created in the divine image. You have a divine mission to accomplish. We all have to increase our acts of goodness and kindness. That is all that's needed to bring the redemption of the entire world."

The transformation left many older Chasidim gasping in the dust. For over a century and a half, Chabad had been about theological contemplation and "labor of the heart." Now, the Rebbe introduced something the likes of which had never been seen before: A worldwide organization dedicated to reaching out to every Jew and pulling them back in.

Not that any of that contemplative, inner labor was ever left behind. It remains the curriculum of every Chabad student. It was simply extended outward, downward, and into the world.

An outside observer would explain simply: These were urgent times. Six million had been lost—even more in Russia—the rate of assimilation in the West was accelerating, and if something drastic wasn't done fast to save world Jewry, there wouldn't be any Jews left to save.

But if you stood at the Rebbe's *farbrengens*—the gatherings at 770 Eastern Parkway, where students and Chasidim would sit or stand for hours and listen to his talks, sing Chasidic melodies, say l'chaim, and listen some more—there you would pick up an entirely different story. The inside story.

"We are the last generation of this exile, the generation to greet Moshiach," the Rebbe would say. "We are gathering the very last sparks, the most concealed and tightly held. We are making the final touches, polishing the buttons. These are the last preparations for a world as it was meant to be. And to do that, you cannot stay within the four walls of your yeshivah or your synagogue. To do that, you must go out into the world, with all your essence and being, and there be a beacon of light, a gatherer of sparks."

Chabad is not two worlds; it is all one, and the only way it can be understood is as a single whole—albeit, working in two opposite directions: from the top-down and from the ground-up. Chabad is about bringing the highest light of the divine to every corner of G-d's world, and it is about discovering and redeeming the divine spark hidden within all that exists.

At one time, that was achieved only in the world of the spirit. In our times, it has become as literal as imaginable.

It's strange—what I am about to say was never stated explicitly, yet all who have been steeped in the Rebbe's world have tacitly understood the same thing. It was implied, again and again, from so many different angles. At some point, it has to be stated loud and clear.

Certainly, every human being on this planet has his or her role to fulfill in its *tikun*. But the Maker of All Souls deemed that a Jewish soul was meant to heal the world with the light of Torah. And that raises a great question. Because, if that is so, why would G-d toss such a soul into a world where she would have no idea that there could be anything spiritual or meaningful to discover in the whole of Judaism?

It could only be that this is the exclusive means to recover those final, lost sparks.

Like a homing pigeon sent on a journey to return with precious jewels, so the souls of Israel are scattered among the nations of the world, among every sort of ideology and idealism, lifestyle and compulsion, ashram and cult, rat-race and escapism. So deep must they plunge that it takes the army of a *tzaddik*, a battalion fighting with all its might, to pull them out of there, so they can bring those jewels back home.

Some sparks can be returned home with a simple mitzvah. Some can only be extracted by cracking a hard nut and tossing out a pile of trash. And some—those "tied down," as Rabbi Schneur Zalman described them—only by exerting every ounce of your strength to pull yourself out of their sticky mud.

There is a teaching that says this—almost:

> *The only reason G-d spread the Jewish People among the nations was so that they could gain converts. As the verse says, "I have planted you among the nations." If a man plants seed, does he not expect to reap a hundred bushels of seed for every bushel planted? (Judges 5:11)*
> —*Talmud Pesachim 87b*

Rabbi Schneur Zalman of Liadi asked, "Can we take this literally? How many converts have there been in history? Could we possibly be in exile from our land for 1,800 years for this reason alone? If this were meant literally, the world should be filled with Jews by now!"

"Rather," he answered, "the converts to which the Talmud refers are none other than the lost sparks. By spreading us out among the nations, we wrestle out those sparks from their place, on their own territory, so that their redemption is a real and lasting one."

Rabbi Schneur Zalman may have seen it, but how many others could have understood how far this would go, to what places we would have to journey to rescue those sparks, how deep those souls would have to plunge to find them, and what extreme means would be needed to convince the homing pigeons to return home.

In 1967, the Rebbe spoke about how the souls had begun to return home. In the 1980s, he talked about the walls of the exile crumbling before us. In 1991, he insisted that enough sparks had been gathered, and it was incomprehensible that the final *geulah* had not yet come.

It was up to us, he said, to complete the job—we had to want it from the innermost of our hearts, and demand it with sincerity. And in order for that to happen, we had to learn what *geulah* is, understand it and come to feel it as though we were living it already. He continued speaking that way until the day of his stroke, in 1992.

In each of our private lives, much work remains to be done. But the world is ready. It is we who must awaken a longing to come home.

If we would recognize what this world really is and who we really are, how high we could be and what a world we could be living in, how we are but silkworms trapped in the darkness of our cocoons, miners trapped in a cave so long that we have forgotten the light of day, a bright, glorious day that awaits us—we would be pounding our fists on heaven's door, demanding to see the fruits of our labor, demanding it now and no later.

In the meantime, keep working. Work hard. For we are G-d's partners in the creation of heaven and earth.

———◆———

About Sources

This list provides sources from the talks, letters and other writings of the Rebbe and his predecessors for further study. It covers most, but not all the contents of this book.

As I wrote in the introduction, while this book contains few direct quotations, its content is firmly grounded in this material. If you are familiar with additional sources that may be useful to other readers, please consider contributing them by email to editor@chabad.org.

Tikun

1. The Drama

2. The Game
Tanya, chs. 36-37. See also Torat Menachem—Hitvaaduyot 5714, vol. 1, p. 228 ff.

3. Completion
Tanya, ch. 37.

4. Write Your Own Script
Torat Menachem—Sefer Hamaamarim Melukat, vol. 1, pp. 181 and 218.

5. The Ultimate Delight
Sefer Hamaamarim Bati Legani, vol. 1, pp. 28-29.

6. If It's Broken…
Avot 2:16. Reshimot, Issue 44.

7. Leave Nothing Behind
Torat Menachem—Hitvaaduyot 5713,

vol. 3, pp. 88-89, and countless other instances.

8. The Soul Grows Up
Likkutei Sichot, vol. 15, p. 249.

9. Descending to Ascend
Torat Menachem—Sefer Hamaamarim Bati Legani, vol. 1, p. 20 ff.

10. Cutting Off the Supply
Tanya, ch. 37.

11. Fearless
Likkutei Sichot, vol. 30, p. 234.

12. Reporting
Tanya, ch. 7, based on Eitz Chaim 26:1. Cited and elucidated in countless talks and writings by the Rebbe.

13. Life's Memories

Meaning

many occasions as a lesson in life (see also Shulchan Aruch, Orach Chaim §276).

31. Come of Days
Likkutei Sichot, vol. 35, p. 91.

32. Counting Time
Torat Menachem—Hitvaaduyot 5742, vol. 3, p. 1192 ff.

33. Life in a Day
Hayom Yom, 17 Cheshvan; Talk of Naso 5737, sec. 6.

34. Arrows of Life
Likkutei Sichot, vol. 5, p. 92.

35. Living Time

36. Balance

37. Fire Burning Fire
Tanya, ch. 3; Sefer Hamaamarim 5710, pp. 112-114.

38. Four Gates
Sefer Hamaamarim 5729, p. 316 ff.

39. Live Clothing
Sefer Hamaamarim 5729, p. 316 ff.; Tanya, chs. 4, 6, 9, 12.

40. Keep the Windows Open
Iggeret Hateshuvah, ch. 1; Torat Menachem—Sefer Hamaamarim Melukat, vol. 1, p. 307 ff.

41. Panic
From a letter.

42. G-d's Image
Torat Menachem—Sefer Hamaamarim Melukat, vol. 2, p. 142 ff.

43. When is G-d?
Torat Menachem—Sefer Hamaamarim Melukat, vol. 2, p. 142 ff.

44. Original Success
Torat Menachem—Sefer Hamaamarim Melukat, vol. 1, p. 246 ff.

45. Crossroads
Torat Menachem—Sefer Hamaamarim Melukat, vol. 2, p. 142 ff.

46. First Day
Torat Menachem—Sefer Hamaamarim Melukat, vol. 1, p. 41 ff.

47. Happy Birthday, Universe
Torat Menachem—Sefer Hamaamarim Melukat, vol. 1, p. 41 ff.; Torat Menachem—Sefer Hamaamarim Melukat, vol. 2, p. 142 ff.

48. Time Travel
Torat Menachem—Sefer Hamaamarim Melukat, vol. 2, p. 142 ff.

49. Two Channels
Igeret Hateshuvah, ch. 6; Torat Menachem—Sefer Hamaamarim Melukat, vol. 3, p. 127 ff.

50. Heaven Desires Earth
Likkutei Sichot, vol. 3, p. 990.

Out in the World

Learn as a Child

Healing Begins At Home

Healing Begins at Home
See Igrot Kodesh, vol. 14, p. 62; see also ibid., vol. 8, p. 58.

85. Harmonization

86. Home Improvement
From a letter dated 12 Menachem Av, 5737.

87. Give & Take
From a letter dated 12 Menachem Av, 5737.

88. Home
Torat Menachem—Hitvaaduyot 5724, vol. 3, pp. 247-248; Talks of Shabbat Vayelech 5732, sec. 5; Shabbat Beshalach 5738, sec. 24; 3rd day Chol Hamoed Sukkot 5741; 24 Elul 5741, sec. 3.

89. Wisdom, Not Hammers
Sefer Hasichot 5704, p. 100.

90. Meditation On a Scolding
To Rabbi Shmuel Lew, in a private audience.

91. Who This Really Is
Likkutei Sichot, vol. 16, p. 321. Torat Menachem—Hitvaaduyot 5745, vol. 3, p. 1544.

92. Unreacting
Igrot Kodesh, vol. 19, p. 75.

93. Blind Love
Derech Mitzvotecha 28a ff.

94. Re-Uniting

95. Getting Personal
Likkutei Sichot, vol. 4, p. 1151.

96. Forgiveness by the Book
Likkutei Sichot, vol. 21, pp. 173-180; ibid., vol. 9, pp. 237-242.

97. A Different Peace
Likkutei Sichot, vol. 18, p. 202 ff.

98. Constant Bonding
Likkutei Sichot, vol., 5, p. 174.

99. Reality in Untidy Boxes

100. The Path of the Humble
Reshimat Nefesh Hashefeilah, cited and elucidated in Likkutei Sichot, vol. 16, p. 41ff. See also Tanya, ch. 27.

101. Imaginary Kindness
Reshimat Nefesh Hashefeilah, cited and elucidated in Likkutei Sichot, vol. 16, p. 41 ff.

about the Rebbe

The Lubavitcher Rebbe, Rabbi Menachem M. Schneerson, was heir to a line of Chasidic Masters that began with the towering figure of the Baal Shem Tov and carried it into the modern day.

With the passing of his father-in-law, Rabbi Yosef Yitzchak Schneersohn, in 1950, after an entire year of petitions and pressure, he accepted the mantle of leadership of what remained of the Chabad-Lubavitch Chasidic sect—a small group of those who had survived the inferno of the Holocaust and the religious persecution of Soviet Russia. Immediately he began to send agents to assist Jewish communities worldwide. In the sixties, he saw in the prevailing spirit of non-conformity, a spiritual reawakening. Through his work, tens of thousands of Jews returned to their roots and their spiritual heritage, as thousands of institutions were established in every part of the globe.

People of all faiths and walks of life travelled from afar to seek his advice and hear his wisdom. Politicians, civil rights activists, writers, scientists, religious leaders, scholars, business people, and any person who sought wisdom and guidance, lined up at his door for many hours every week. Sacks of mail arrived daily with requests for guidance and blessings from every corner of the world.

His talks and letters covered a wide gamut of topics, from the most esoteric teachings of Kabbalah and the nuances of Talmudic debate to his concerns over public school education in America and the safety of those living in Israel. In his signature style, everything had to have a practical application.

In 1978, on his 76th birthday, Congress proclaimed Rabbi Schneerson's birthday as, "Education Day, USA," and subsequently awarded the Rebbe the National Scroll of Honor.

In 1995, the Rebbe was posthumously awarded the Congressional Gold Medal, an award granted to only 130 Americans since Thomas Jefferson, for "outstanding and lasting contributions."

This book offers every person an opportunity to connect with the Rebbe through his teachings, condensed from over 50 years of letters, public talks, private conversations, and written works, presented in an accessible format.

about the author

Rabbi Tzvi Freeman was born in Vancouver, Canada, where he became involved at an early age in Yoga, Tao, and radical politics. In 1975, he left a career as a classical guitarist and composer to study Talmud and Jewish mysticism for nine years.

He is a senior editor at Chabad.org, for which he writes the *Daily Dose of Wisdom*, from which the meditations of this volume were extracted. He also directs the Chabad.org *Ask-the-Rabbi* team and produces *KabbalaToons*, a series of short, animated videos starring Rabbi Infinity.

His other books include:
- Bringing Heaven Down To Earth, Book I
- Bringing Heaven Down To Earth, Book II
- Heaven Exposed
- Men, Women & Kabala
- Trembling With Joy